Our Earth

Weather and Seasons

Jen Green

WAYLAND

First published in 2007 by Wayland
Copyright © Wayland 2007

Wayland
338 Euston Road
London NW1 3BH

Wayland Australia
Hachette Children's Books
Level 17/207 Kent Street
Sydney NSW 2000

Produced by Tall Tree Ltd
Editor: Jon Richards
Designer: Ben Ruocco
Consultant: John Williams

British Library Cataloguing in Publication
Data
 Green, Jen
   Weather & seasons. – (Our Earth)
   1. Weather – Juvenile literature 2. Seasons
   – Juvenile literature
   I. Title
   551.6

   ISBN-13: 9780750250078

Printed in China
Wayland is a division of Hachette
Children's Books.

Picture credits:
Cover Dreamstime.com/Brian Grant,
1 and 12 Dreamstime.com/Jerry Horn,
4 Dreamstime.com, 5 Dreamstime.com/
Martine Oger, 6 Dreamstime.com/Andre
Klopper, 7 Dreamstime.com/Ernest Prim,
8 Dreamstime.com/Cora Reed,
9 Dreamstime.com, 10 Alamy/David Young-
Wolff, 11 Dreamstime.com/Rene Waerts,
13 Dreamstime.com/Brian Grant,
14 Alamy/Zute Lightfoot, 15 Alamy/F. Jack
Jackson, 16 Dreamstime.com, 17 Digital
Vision, 18 Alamy/nagelestock.com,
19 Dreamstime.com/Bernard Breton,
20 NASA, 21 AP Photo/Weather
Underground

Contents

What is weather?

Weather is what happens to the air outside. The air may be hot or cold. This can give us sunny, windy, cloudy or rainy weather. Weather can change as clouds cover a blue sky or the Sun shines.

On the beach we wear clothes that keep us cool. Sun cream protects us from the Sun's rays.

⬥ Playing in the snow is fun if you are wearing the right clothes to keep you warm.

Weather is important in our daily lives. It affects the clothes we wear, how we travel about, the food we eat and how we live.

Blowing winds

Wind is the movement of air. The Sun's heat makes the air move. When warm air heated by the Sun rises, cold air moves in to take its place. This movement of air is wind. Winds bring changes in the weather.

▼ Kites fly best on breezy days when the wind keeps them in the air.

Hurricanes are powerful **storms** with winds that can blow down buildings and cause lots of damage.

Winds may be light or strong. A light breeze moves the leaves on the branch of a tree. A strong wind tosses whole branches. A very strong wind can blow down a tree or rip tiles off a roof.

Cloudy days

When the Sun heats the ocean, water
rises as a gas called water vapour.
High in the sky where the air is cold,
the gas turns back to drops of water
to make clouds.

❯❯ The water and
ice gather
together to
make clouds.

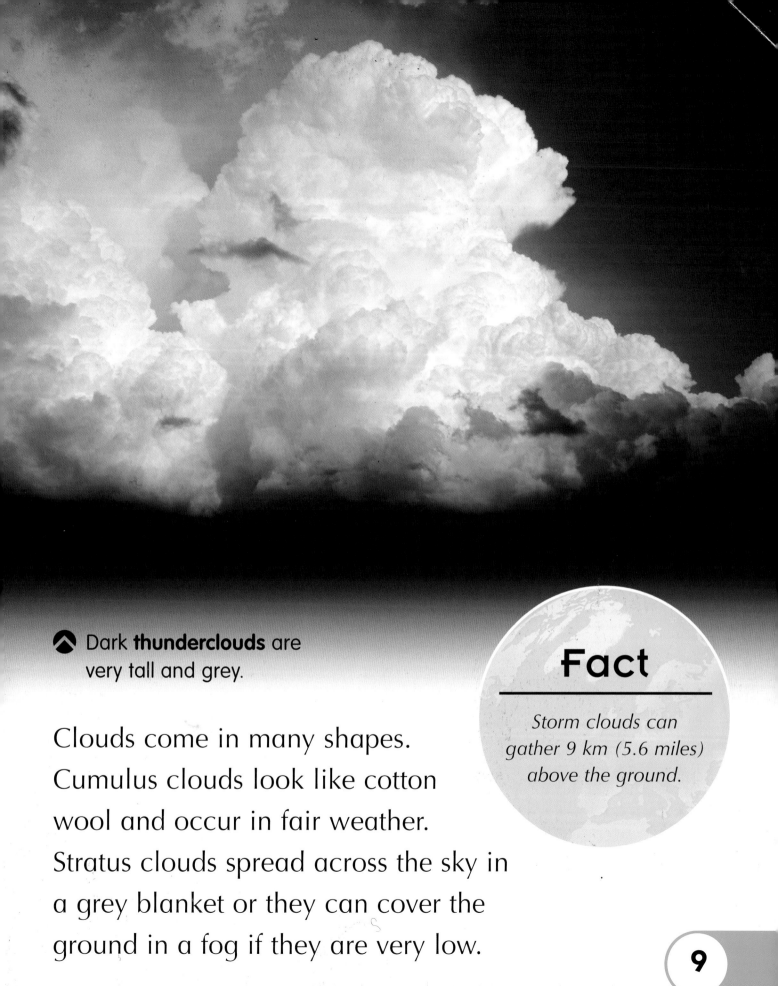

🔺 Dark **thunderclouds** are
very tall and grey.

Clouds come in many shapes.
Cumulus clouds look like cotton
wool and occur in fair weather.
Stratus clouds spread across the sky in
a grey blanket or they can cover the
ground in a fog if they are very low.

Fact

*Storm clouds can
gather 9 km (5.6 miles)
above the ground.*

Rain and snow

The tiny drops of water that make up clouds are blown around by the wind. They bump together and join to make bigger drops. The drops become heavy and fall as rain.

⬇ We use umbrellas in the rain. They are **waterproof**.

10

Snow covers the ground until the temperature warms up and the snow melts.

Fact

In Cherrapunji, India, 9.3 m (30.5 ft) of rain fell in one month during the **monsoon** of 1861.

In very cold air, the water in clouds turns to ice. Ice crystals join to make snowflakes. When the weather is cold, the snow falls and covers the ground.

Storms

Thunderstorms can happen in the summer. Inside the dark thunderclouds, water droplets and ice crystals rub together. The rubbing produces **electricity**.

⌄ Light travels faster than sound, so you see the lightning before you hear the thunder.

The electricity is released as a streak of lightning. The massive spark heats the air so quickly it explodes. You hear this explosion as a loud crash of thunder.

Fact

Inside a tornado, winds blow at up to 500 km/h (300 mph).

▼ **Tornadoes** are storms with funnels of spinning air. Inside these funnels are powerful winds that suck up objects as the tornadoes move.

World weather

Climate is the type of weather a place has over a long period of time. Different parts of the world have different climates. The part of the Earth around the Equator is called the **tropics.**

⊗ Places in the tropics are hot because the Sun beats down directly from above.

◀ Snow and ice cover the polar regions for all or most of the year.

At the **poles**, the Sun is always low in the sky so its rays are weaker. These places are always cold. **Temperate** regions lie between the tropics and the poles. They have a mild climate that is neither too hot nor too cold.

The seasons

Weather changes throughout the year. These changes are called the **seasons**. Many areas have four seasons. These are spring, summer, autumn and winter.

⊗ Most animals have their young in spring, as the weather starts to get warmer.

❯❯ In autumn, leaves turn red or orange before they fall to the ground.

Fact

Some animals eat lots of food in the autumn and then sleep through winter. This is called **hibernation***.*

Winter is the coldest season. In spring, leaves start to appear on trees and the days get longer. Summer is the warmest season. In autumn, the days get shorter and the weather starts to get colder.

What causes the seasons?

The seasons happen because the Earth tilts as it spins and moves around the Sun. During the summer, the part of the Earth where you live leans toward the Sun. In winter, your part of the Earth leans away from the Sun.

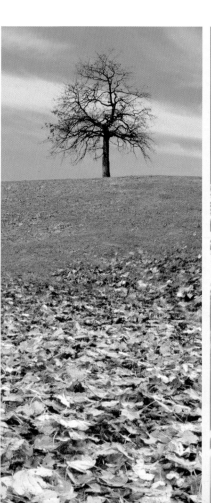 In spring, plants start to grow. After summer, the weather gets cooler and many plants die or lose their leaves before the cold of winter.

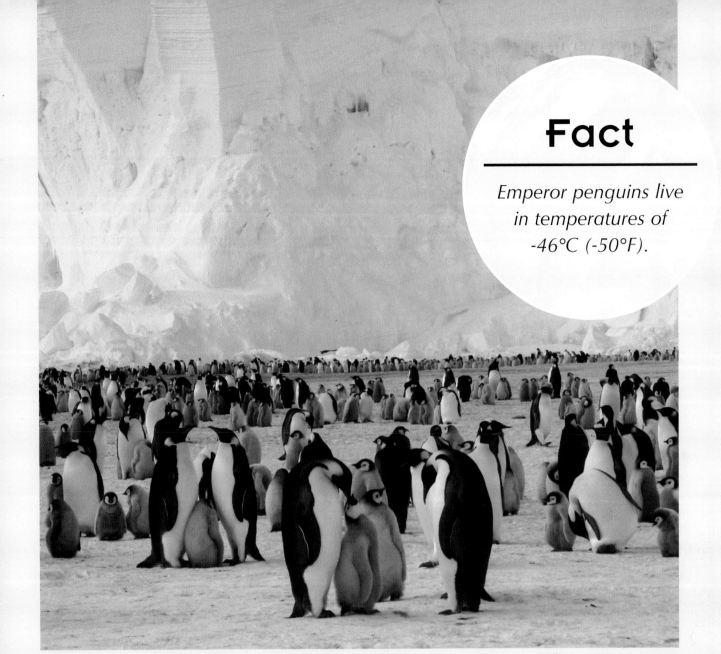

The seasons affect many animals and birds. Some birds and animals travel to warmer areas for the winter. This is called **migration**.

Polar animals, such as penguins, have thick feathers or fur to keep them warm in the cold climate.

Tomorrow's weather

What will the weather be like tomorrow? **Weather forecasts** help us to see any changes in the weather. Many people rely on weather forecasts for their work.

⊻ This picture taken from space shows a spinning hurricane.

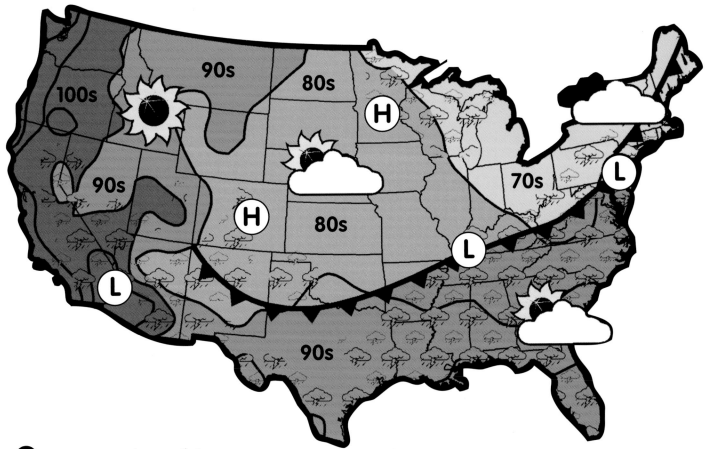

⬆ Maps such as this one show tomorrow's weather. Can you see the signs for cloud and sunshine?

Experts gather information from **weather stations**. The information is fed into computers, which help to produce maps and weather forecasts.

Fact

There are over 50,000 weather stations around the world, some are even in space.

Activities

Make waves in a bowl

Waves are made by wind blowing over the sea. Make your own waves and record the results.

WHAT YOU NEED

- **Bowl with a broad rim**
- **Jug of water**
- **Paper**
- **Pencil**

1. Fill the bowl with water and put it near the edge of a table.

2. Sit down so that you can bring your mouth close to the bowl.

3. Blow gently over the bowl. Look at the wave patterns on the water's surface. Sketch the wave patterns.

4. Blow harder and draw the patterns again. Compare the two patterns.

Sketch the patterns you see on the water.

Making a weather vane

Make your own **weather vane** to find out which way the wind is blowing.

WHAT YOU NEED

- **Two pieces of card cut into triangles of different sizes**
- **Pair of scissors**
- **Two plastic straws**
- **Sticky tape**
- **Modelling clay**
- **Empty cotton reel**

12 cm

10 cm

12 cm

4 cm

4 cm

4 cm

4 cm

1. Stick the small triangle to one end of a straw and the large triangle to the other end of the same straw.

Use sticky tape to hold cards in place.

Use a lump of clay to fix one straw to the other.

2. Use the modelling clay to fix the other straw to the middle of the first straw and push this through the cotton reel. On a breezy day, hold your weather vane and watch it point to where the wind is coming from.